Healthy L

**Stop Picky Eating Before it Starts:
Your Guide to Feeding Babies and Toddlers**

Tera Naset, MS, RD

Healthy Little Foodie

Copyright © 2019, Tera Naset
First Edition

All rights reserved

www.teranasetnutrition.com

ISNB 978-1-7332569-0-2

Healthy Little Foodie is intended solely for informational and educational purposes and not as personal medical advice. Always seek personalized advice from licensed medical professionals to answer any questions you have regarding a medical condition before undertaking any diet, exercise or other health program.

The information in this book is not intended to treat, diagnose, cure or prevent any disease. The approach proposed in this book is not sponsored, approved, recommended or endorsed by the FDA, USDA, NIH, ADA, AND or any other organization.

Cover Design: Tera Naset
Layout & Formatting: Tera Naset

UNENDING THANKS

Being in a position to advise others, particularly on a topic so personal, is not an opportunity that I take lightly. I would not be able to do so without the unending support I have received from so many people.

Thanks especially to my parents, Frank and Doreen, for encouraging me to follow my passion for food even if it meant abandoning the business career they originally championed.

And to my husband, John, for enduring life with a dietitian and all of the grocery shopping, cooking and countless discussions about food that come with it.

To my children, Madeleine and Francis, my muses, my inspiration – I hope your life is delicious and nutritious every step of the way.

And finally, to the adult patients with whom I have spent my career thus far. My biggest regret is not meeting you sooner. No one should have to struggle with the preventable diseases that are decimating our population today. You were let down by a broken system, set up to fail. My greatest hope is that together we can establish a new normal when it comes to food. Children are our future, and this is our chance to make the future brighter.

TABLE OF CONTENTS

INTRODUCTION

Confession: I have spent my career as a dietitian treating adults, not kids. I actually intended to go into pediatrics, but as fate would have it, I landed a job after graduation in adult weight management and just never left. I have treated patients looking to lose anywhere from 10 pounds to hundreds. Many are battling advanced chronic diseases like diabetes and heart disease. They are usually on at least three or four medications for metabolic disease, some of which are horribly expensive and may even require daily injections. To be frank, their quality of life is abysmal and there is only so much that anyone can do. I leave work every evening wondering how we got here. How did it come to pass that more than 100 million American have diabetes or prediabetes, and one in five school-aged children is obese?[1,2] The answer to that question is complex, but there is no doubt that much of the trouble starts in childhood. Even among the 80% of kids who do not develop overt childhood obesity, the standard American diet is quietly wreaking havoc on their innocent little bodies. By the time they come to me as adults, the damage is done.

As both a dietitian and a mom, I cannot stand idly by and watch the demise of human health. We need to help kids develop a healthy relationship with "adult" food instead of bland or hyper-sweet "kid" foods that set them up for a lifetime of unhealthy habits. It is a common misconception that food lovers, or "foodies," become overweight due to overindulgence. In reality, the vast majority of overweight adults that I treat actually consider themselves "picky" eaters. Processed foods are designed to be only moderately flavorful and thus appealing to picky palates. In fact, food scientists work hard to ensure that processed foods are not overly flavorful – their goal is for each bite to leave you wanting a little bit more.[3] This, of course, leads to higher sales for the food companies...and weight gain for the consumers! Real, robustly flavored food is just the opposite. Strong flavors such as bleu cheese, dark chocolate and balsamic vinegar are satisfying in much smaller quantities. By raising kids to enjoy these adult flavors, we can set them up for a lifetime of delicious and appropriate eating habits. This is a mission that starts on day one and never ends. This guide focuses on the first years of a child's life, but many of the themes are applicable throughout childhood. Families that shop, cook and eat together stay healthy together. It's as simple as that.

EQUIPMENT

There is no need to buy special equipment to make baby food. Companies love to market expensive contraptions solely for this purpose, but standard kitchen equipment will work just fine, or better! As long as you have the short list of items below, you will be all set!

- LARGE FOOD PROCESSOR. A food processor is absolutely critical for most of the purees in this book. Look for one with at least a 7-cup capacity.

- SMALL FOOD PROCESSOR. A second, smaller food processor is not strictly necessary, but is nice if you want to avoid dragging out the bigger food processor for some of the smaller volume recipes. A 3-cup or 21-ounce capacity is a good size.

- SLOW COOKER. A slow cooker is great for making meat purees. Cooking meat low and slow will break down tough connective tissue, making the meat easy to puree. It also works well for tenderizing veggies and cooking beans. If you do not already have one, slow cookers are a workhorse in the family kitchen, guaranteed to get tons of use well beyond the baby food days.

- SILICONE FREEZER TRAYS. Many purees are easiest to make in large batches. By freezing them in small portions, you can defrost just what you need over the course of a few months. Standard plastic ice cube trays can be used, but silicone trays are much easier to work with. Look for ones that make portions around the size of a standard ice cube, about half an ounce to an ounce per cube. They are often marketed as "silicone candy molds" or "silicone ice cube trays."

Quick Guide

This book is jam-packed with details about exactly when, how and why to feed your baby certain foods. Below is a quick timeline outlining the basic strategy. Ages are based on full-term babies. If your baby was born prematurely, you may need to use his/her corrected age to determine the most suitable stage of development.

0–6 Months	The Milk Months	Breast milk and/or formula are the only things a baby needs up until around six months old. Starting complimentary foods too early can cause digestive upset and poses the risk of aspiration (sucking food into the airway). It has also been correlated with obesity later in life.[4]
4–5 Months	First Sips	After four months old, you may opt to include very small amounts of cod liver oil and bone broth.[5] Offer just ¼ teaspoon of cod liver oil and a few sips of bone broth daily to avoid any decrease in milk consumption. These supplements can be continued throughout life. The cod liver oil especially makes a great family supplement – increase to the full dosage as noted on the package around three years of age.

| 6–8 Months | Perfect Purees | Most babies are ready for purees around six months old. Signs of readiness include the ability to sit in a high chair without slouching over and a willingness to take purees into their mouth without automatically thrusting them out with their tongue.[6]

There is no need to introduce foods one at a time unless there is a family history of allergies. However, it is a good idea to offer new foods at breakfast or lunch rather than dinner so that you can monitor baby after eating.

Begin spoon-feeding 1–2 tablespoons of meat or fish puree and 1–2 tablespoons of a vegetable or fruit puree at a minimum of two meals per day. Try to offer vegetables instead of fruit at least half the time.

Sample Schedule with Three Naps
7:00 am – Wake, nurse or bottle
7:30 am – Breakfast (can skip if feeding at lunch and dinner)
9:00 am – Nap
10:30 am – Nurse or bottle
12:00 pm – Lunch (can skip if feeding at breakfast and dinner)
12:30 pm – Nap
2:00 pm – Nurse or bottle
4:30 pm – Nap
5:00 pm – Nurse or bottle
6:00 pm – Dinner (can skip if feeding at breakfast and lunch)
6:30 pm – Nurse or bottle |
|---|---|---|

7:00 pm – Asleep for the night
1:00 am – Optional nursing session or bottle.
Most babies outgrow the need for night
feedings between six and eight months old

Sample Schedule with Two Naps
7:00 am – Wake, nurse or bottle
7:30 am – Breakfast (can skip if feeding at
lunch and dinner)
9:00 am – Nap
11:00 am – Nurse or bottle
12:00 pm – Lunch (can skip if feeding at
breakfast and dinner)
2:00 pm – Nap
4:00 pm – Nurse or bottle
6:00 pm – Dinner (can skip if feeding at
breakfast and lunch)
6:30 pm – Nurse or bottle
7:00 pm – Asleep for the night
1:00 am – Optional nursing session or bottle.
Most babies outgrow the need for night
feedings between six and eight months old

9–12 Months	Finger Foods	Most babies develop their pincer grasp around nine months old. This is the ability to pick up small pieces of food with their thumb and forefinger. With this new skill comes the opportunity to self-feed. You can continue to offer purees if desired, but start to incorporate some finger foods at each meal.
		This is the ideal time to align baby's meals with your family's meals. Aim to feed baby three times a day, ideally at the same times you eat. Pull their high chair as close to the table as you can, scatter some finger food on the tray and let them eat while watching you enjoy your meal. Babies are great imitators, so they tend to enjoy their food more if they see you enjoying yours rather than focusing on them, watching like a hawk.
		Meat, fish, vegetables and fruit are still great options. This is also a great time to add foods that do not lend themselves to purees such as eggs, cheese, nuts, beans and whole grains. You can even chop up small pieces of whatever the rest of the family is eating.
		Follow your baby's cues with regard to how much food to offer. Since they are self-feeding, it is unlikely that they would overeat. It is also OK if they do not seem to be eating much at all. This is an exploratory time for babies. They are still getting most of their nutrition from milk, so the main goal of feeding is to get them accustomed to various flavors and textures in time for their first

birthday, when food will take over as the main source of nutrition.

Begin offering water in a children's cup at meals around 11 months. This will prepare baby to drink milk at meals after age one. When selecting a children's cup, opt for straw-based or open cups instead of traditional sippy cups to promote proper muscle development in the mouth.

Sample Schedule with Two Naps
7:00 am – Wake, nurse or bottle
7:30 am – Breakfast
9:00 am – Nap
11:00 am – Nurse or bottle
12:00 pm – Lunch
2:00 pm – Nap
4:00 pm – Nurse or bottle
6:00 pm – Dinner
6:30 pm – Nurse or bottle
7:00 pm – Asleep for the night

Note that no snacks are offered. Only offer food at the three mealtimes. Between three meals and four bottles and/or nursing sessions, baby will be eating often enough.

| 12+ Months | | Around 12 months, you can stop preparing "baby food" for your child, who is now a toddler and can join the family table. Toddlers may still need their food cut into small, manageable pieces, but they should be able to eat the same food as the rest of the family. If possible, transition to a high chair or booster seat that allows them to actually sit at the table. Otherwise, simply push their high chair as close as possible.

At this point, you can begin offering whole milk in a children's straw cup or open cup *with* meals, instead of nursing or providing bottles throughout the day. If you would like to continue nursing after baby's first birthday, nurse after meals instead of before so that he/she will not be too full of milk to eat solid food. Over time, you should transition to offering water at one or two meals instead of milk.

Sample Schedule with Two Naps
*This schedule is ideal for new one-year-olds because it still incorporates a large quantity of whole cow's milk or breast milk.
7:00 am – Wake
7:30 am – Breakfast. Offer whole milk or nurse immediately after
9:00 am – Nap
12:00 pm – Lunch. Offer whole milk or nurse immediately after
2:00 pm – Nap
4:00 pm – Optional snack
6:00 pm – Dinner. Offer whole milk or nurse immediately after |

7:00 pm – Asleep for the night

Sample Schedule with One Nap
*This schedule is ideal for older one-year-olds, starting around 15 months, because it emphasizes water instead of whole cow's milk or breast milk.
7:00 am – Wake
7:30 am – Breakfast. Offer water. Optional: offer whole milk or nurse immediately after
11:30 am – Lunch. Offer water. Optional: offer whole milk or nurse immediately after
12:00 pm – Nap.
4:00 pm – Optional snack
6:00 pm – Dinner. Offer water. Optional: offer whole milk or nurse immediately after
7:00 pm – Asleep for the night

Note that there is only one snack and it is optional. It is critical that toddlers arrive at meals hungry. Toddlers who snack often or drink milk between meals may appear to be "picky" eaters when in reality they are simply not hungry enough to try something new.

THE MILK MONTHS (0–6 MONTHS)

I n a lot of ways, the milk months are the best months, especially for foodie parents. When my daughter was a newborn, we would tote her along everywhere. With no sleep schedule and only one life-sustaining fluid, she could join us at restaurants, sporting events, bars and everywhere in between. Sure, these are also the sleepless months, but cherish them nonetheless. Before you know it, you will be eating dinner at 5:00 pm and apologizing as your toddler throws burrata at the restaurant wall.

BREAST MILK

Not surprisingly, breast milk is the superior milk choice from a nutrition standpoint.[7] Made specifically for human babies, it contains the precise combination of nutrients they need in addition to antibodies that help fight off illness. For moms who are able to nurse their babies directly, there is an added benefit of helping babies learn their own fullness cues. Because breastfeeding takes more effort on baby's part, most babies will only eat until they are full. On the contrary, parents are often able to cajole bottle-fed babies into eating more than they need with a "just finish this bottle" mentality.

But perhaps even more interesting is the fact that mom's diet can actually change the flavor of the milk. Research shows that in the hours after a meal, breast milk will take on the flavor of whatever mom ate. This is great news for foodie moms trying to give their baby's palate a head start!

FORMULA

The fact of the matter is, most babies in America today will receive some baby formula at some point. According to the Centers for Disease Control and Prevention, 81% of babies start out breastfeeding, but by six months, only 22% are still exclusively breastfed.[8] This means at least 78% of babies receive formula by six months of age, and still more do by 12 months of age. But in spite of its popularity, many of the bestselling formulas on the market are far from ideal for young palates and bodies.

From a nutrition perspective, formula should mimic breast milk as closely as possible. Because cow's milk, the basis for most formulas, differs greatly from human milk, certain elements must be added or removed in order to achieve this. Protein ratios are altered, certain fats and sugars added and mineral levels adjusted. Most companies are fairly adept at these alterations, but they do have to make a few key choices along the way.

MILK QUALITY

Since the main ingredient in most baby formula is cow's milk, it stands to reason that we should care about the quality of the milk. The absolute ideal is milk from 100% grass-fed cows. This concept is slowly but surely permeating the formula world. In Germany, a number of brands use grass-fed milk, as do many in Australia. HiPP and Holle are the most popular and fairly easy to obtain abroad. A few US brands are getting on board as well.

If grass-fed cow's milk is not an option, the next best thing is an organic formula. This implies that the cows were fed grain and soy, which is unfortunate, but that the feed was organic and not genetically modified. A number of brands offer organic formulas.

SWEETENERS

Perhaps the most concerning issue with trying to make formula more similar to breast milk is sugar. It is true that breast milk contains more lactose, a mildly sweet-tasting sugar, than cow's milk. But rather than simply adding additional lactose to cow's milk, most manufacturers choose lower-cost, more readily available types of sugar. These alternatives can be substantially sweeter than lactose. As a result, babies become accustomed to very sweet flavors. This may account for the recent scourge of toddlers deemed "picky eaters," refusing all but very sweet, starchy foods. In addition, some researchers hypothesize that very sweet formulas may be addicting, causing babies to override their internal satiety cues and consume more formula than is necessary.

The best way to determine a formula's sweetness is to read the ingredients. All formulas will list some sort of added sugar within the first three or four ingredients. The table below lists the sweetness index for various sugars. A value of 1 is given to sucrose, which is table sugar. You will see that lactose, the sugar naturally found in cow's milk and breast milk, has a value of 0.15. This means it has less than one fifth the sweetness of table sugar. When evaluating a formula, look for one that uses a sugar with a lower value on the sweetness index.

Sugar	Sweetness Index
Lactose	0.15
Maltodextrin	0.15
Maltose	0.3
Brown Rice Syrup	0.5
Glucose/Dextrose/Corn Syrup	0.75
Sucrose	1.0
High Fructose Corn Syrup	1.2

So, if you find yourself in the formula aisle, take a deep breath and know that you *can* find good options for your baby. Take your time, read the ingredients and make the best choice you can.

FIRST SIPS (4–5 MONTHS)

Months four and five are still technically "milk months." There is no nutritional need for table food before baby's six month birthday. However, two special liquids can be introduced at this time: cod liver oil and bone broth. In many ways these serve as supplements, but unlike most modern supplements, they are simple foods instead of chemically derived supplement products.

COD LIVER OIL

Vitamin D supplementation is recommended for all breastfed infants and many formula-fed infants. Currently the American Academy of Pediatrics recommends a total intake of 400 IU/day for infants and children.[9] It is important to note that vitamin D research is ongoing and these recommendations change frequently. Regardless, there is merit to the idea that many people, adults and kids alike, may now be deficient in this critical vitamin.

The absolute best way to obtain vitamin D is through direct exposure to sunlight without sunscreen or protective clothing.[10] Unfortunately our modern indoor lifestyle, combined with concerns about skin cancer, has greatly reduced our ability to obtain vitamin D from the sun. Luckily we are not the first generation of humans to face this issue. Native populations in the far northern regions of the world have always faced long, dark winters. Their solution is one we can still use today: cod liver oil.

Cod liver oil is extracted from the liver of the codfish. Reputable cod liver oil producers do not add or subtract any substance from the pure oil. Therefore, all of its nutrients occur in natural ratios, as they do in food. This makes the vitamin D found in liquid cod liver oil much more functional than that found in the baby vitamin D drops that are typically recommended. Three reputable brands to consider are NutraPro, Rosita and Carlson. Most babies are happy to take unflavored cod liver oil, but if the whole family would like to share one bottle, consider flavored varieties.

Parents can begin offering cod liver oil when baby is four or five months old. Try spoon-feeding 1/4 teaspoon of the oil while baby is sitting in a high chair or on a parent's lap. Alternatively, you can use an eye dropper or small syringe to squeeze the oil into the corner of baby's mouth. Once the child is around three years old, you can increase to the full dosage recommended on the package.

BONE BROTH

Bone broth is just a fancy name for water that has been boiled with animal bones. This time-tested tradition dates back to the Stone Age, millennia before the complicated science of nutrition was unearthed.[11] Once upon a time, people just knew instinctively that no part of the animal should be wasted and that water boiled with bones is tastier and more nutritious than plain water.

Today, most people only consume bone broth, also known as stock, as a base for soups or sauces. But it offers rich, satisfying nutrition all on its own. When the bones are simmered over many hours, they begin to release their collagen. Collagen is further broken down into gelatin, which is protein that contains 19 different amino acids. One of the most predominant is the amino acid glycine, which plays a critical role in growth and development.[12] Gelatin also assists with digestion, particularly of milk products, and can be especially helpful for infants who need help digesting baby formula. In addition, bone broths made with ample vegetables in addition to bones contain a variety of minerals such as calcium, copper, iron, magnesium, manganese, phosphorus, potassium, sodium and zinc.

You can offer bone broth to baby via a bottle or sippy cup. Just a few tablespoons a day goes a long way. At this age, milk is still the main source of nutrition, and you do not want to displace too much volume with broth. Because of its gelatin content, bone broth may become jellied when refrigerated. You can gently warm it in a bottle warmer, on the stove or in the microwave until it liquefies.

If you are not interested in making bone broth, a number of high-quality products are available for purchase. Look for brands that use 100% grass-fed animal bones and have ingredient lists that are simple and straightforward.

CHICKEN OR TURKEY STOCK

Poultry stock has a mild, pleasant flavor. It is the perfect way to use the carcass of a roasted chicken or the bones left over from Thanksgiving dinner. If possible, try to find pasture-raised poultry. Organic poultry is a good alternative.

Ingredients

- 1 chicken carcass, or about 2 pounds of turkey bones (include the neck and/or feet, if available)
- 1 tablespoon apple cider vinegar
- 3 celery stalks, broken into large chunks (optional)
- 3 large carrots, broken into large chunks (optional)
- 1 medium yellow onion, skin on, roughly chopped (optional)
- Water to fill the slow cooker

Preparation

1. Place the bones in a 5- to 8-quart slow cooker. Drizzle the apple cider vinegar over the bones. Add the vegetables, if using. Fill to the top with water.
2. Cook on low for 12 hours.
3. Use a large colander to strain the broth into a large heat-proof bowl. Cover and allow to cool on the counter for 1 hour before transferring to the refrigerator for at least 8 hours or overnight.
4. Use stock within 1 week or freeze for up to 6 months. To freeze small portions, use an ice cube tray or small silicone molds. Once frozen, cubes can be popped out of the tray/mold and stored in freezer bags or containers.

BEEF STOCK

Beef stock has a much more pronounced flavor than chicken stock. It also has a much higher fat and gelatin content and is extremely nutritious. If possible, try to find grass-fed beef bones for your stock.

Ingredients

- 2 pounds beef bones, ideally a variety of bone types such as joint bones and long bones
- 1 tablespoon apple cider vinegar
- 3 celery stalks, broken into large chunks (optional)
- 3 large carrots, broken into large chunks (optional)
- 1 medium yellow onion, skin on, roughly chopped (optional)
- Water to fill the slow cooker

Preparation

1. Preheat the oven to 450°F. Place the bones on a baking sheet and roast for 1 hour. If desired, you can line the baking sheet with foil for easier cleanup.
2. Place the roasted bones in a 5- to 8-quart slow cooker. Drizzle the apple cider vinegar over the bones. Add the vegetables, if using. Fill to the top with water.
3. Cook on low for 12 to 24 hours. The broth will become more intensely flavored the longer it simmers.
4. Use a large colander to strain the broth into a large heat-proof bowl. Cover and allow to cool on the counter for 1 hour before transferring to the refrigerator for at least 8 hours or overnight.

5. After refrigeration, a fat cap will rise to the top of the bowl and solidify. Use a spatula to lift it off and discard, or save for other uses.
6. Use stock within 1 week or freeze for up to 6 months. To freeze small portions, use an ice cube tray or small silicone molds. Once frozen, cubes can be popped out of the tray/mold and stored in freezer bags or containers.

PERFECT PUREES (6+ MONTHS)

You made it! For many foodie parents, the six-month mark is the most exciting milestone in the first year. It is also one of the most controversial moments in the feeding realm. Many pediatricians still recommend baby cereal as the first food of choice. Yet, popular media regularly touts foods such as avocado and banana, or perhaps the concept of baby-led weaning, starting kids off with a chicken leg or whole apple! What's a well-intentioned food-loving parent to do?

A combination of science, logic and caution went into the recommendations you will find here. They will almost certainly differ from most pediatricians' recommendations, and may sound different from what you heard from a friend. But I urge you to favor science, logic and caution and give them a try. In fact, let baby be the judge; you might just be surprised – although perhaps not as surprised as my daughter's daycare teacher when she showed up with homemade liver pâté for lunch!

BABY-LED WEANING

This book is organized based on the most common progression: spoon-fed purees from about six to eight months old, followed by finger foods starting around nine months. This progression is based on a developmental milestone called the pincer grasp. Around nine months, babies develop the ability to pick up foods between their thumb and forefinger. This allows them to eat foods that are cut into small pieces, thus avoiding a choking risk. Some babies love purees and do very well with this standard progression. However, it is not unheard of for certain babies to reject spoon-feeding. These independent kids may be better suited for the "baby-led weaning" technique.[13] In this approach, you start at six months with soft foods in the shape of sticks or balls, such as cooked green beans or meatballs. These foods are easy to grasp in the fist and chew with just gums. If this method seems like a better fit for your baby, the recipes in the next chapter, Finger Foods, are a great place to start. Most can be served in a stick or ball shape for younger babies or cut into smaller pieces for older babies who have mastered the pincer grasp. Keep in mind, you can certainly do a combination of purees and baby-led weaning starting at six months. You might find that some of your family meals lend themselves nicely to baby self-feeding, while others do not. You could offer the family meal when it works well, and purees when it does not.

PACKAGED BABY FOOD

You have probably noticed that the grocery store has an entire aisle dedicated to baby food purees. You have also probably noticed that being a parent is time-consuming and tiring. So perhaps this aisle appeals to you. That's OK! Babies only eat purees for two to three months, so do what makes sense for your family. Read through this section to get an idea of what foods to introduce, in what order and why. Then feel free to glaze over the actual recipes and just purchase store-bought versions of these purees. If possible, consider buying organic brands to ensure higher quality meat and produce. You might even want to jazz up some of the store-bought purees with the flavors you will find in these recipes. Some baby food companies are getting more adventurous with seasonings, but most of the products on the shelf are super bland. Feel free to add a pinch of salt, some garlic, herbs, cinnamon – you name it! Add flavors that sound good to you and start molding your tiny little foodie's palate.

ALLERGENS

Introduction of allergens has been a controversial topic in recent years. For a long time, parents were warned to withhold common allergens, especially peanuts, until their baby turned one. Newer research has shown that introducing allergens early can actually reduce the incidence of allergic reaction, especially in kids with risk factors such as eczema, other known food allergies or a family history of food allergies.[14] The top eight food allergens are milk, eggs, fish, shellfish, nuts, peanuts, wheat and soybeans. Many of these foods are incorporated into the recipes that follow. In order to err on the side of caution, I recommend offering the top allergens for the first two or three times at a meal that is not immediately followed by sleep. This way you can monitor your child for any reaction. You can also avoid serving two new allergens at the same time, which helps to identify the culprit if there is a reaction. For example, my whipped salmon recipe contains both dairy (yogurt) and fish (salmon). Do not offer this puree unless baby has already tried either dairy or fish in the past, with no reaction. That way, if there is a reaction, you will know it's to the one that he or she had not yet tried.

MEAT

At six months, most babies will begin to run out of the iron they stored up during gestation.[15] Breast milk does not contain much iron, so it is critical that the diet expand to include iron-rich foods. However, breast milk or formula *does* still provide the vast majority of a six-month-old's nutrition, and we do not want them to fill up on food and reduce their milk intake at this point.

It is worth noting that there are two types of iron: heme and non-heme. Heme iron is much easier to absorb, and thus we need less of it to satisfy our body's needs.[16] Babies have incredibly small stomachs, so a smaller quantity of easily absorbed iron makes logical sense.

Baby cereal contains very little naturally occurring iron; instead, it is fortified with non-heme iron during manufacturing. What baby cereal *does* naturally contain is a lot of very filling carbohydrate. And because the non-heme iron is so poorly absorbed, a relatively large volume of cereal is needed to fulfill baby's iron needs. On the contrary, meat contains high amounts of naturally occurring heme iron. A small amount of meat can go a long way, while expanding baby's palate and leaving space for critical breast milk or formula. Thus, I recommend high-quality meat as baby's first food.

* *

BABY POT ROAST
Beef is a great place to start, thanks to its high iron content. If at all possible, try to find 100% grass-fed beef. If this is not available, organic beef is the next best option. Keep in mind that a few pounds of stew meat will amount to a very large amount of pureed beef, so the higher price will go a long way.

Ingredients

- 1 medium yellow onion, sliced
- 2 celery stalks, sliced
- 2 large carrots, peeled and sliced
- 2 to 3 pounds beef stew meat, cubed
- 1 teaspoon salt
- 1 teaspoon garlic powder
- 1/2 teaspoon dried thyme
- 1/2 teaspoon dried parsley
- 1/4 teaspoon black pepper
- 1 cup water
- 2 tablespoons tomato paste

Preparation

1. Arrange the onion, celery and carrots in the bottom of a slow cooker.
2. Place the stew meat in a large bowl. In a small bowl, combine the salt, garlic powder, thyme, parsley and pepper. Sprinkle over the meat and toss to combine well. Add the meat to the slow cooker on top of the veggies.
3. Whisk together the water and the tomato paste until well combined. Pour over the beef.
4. Cook on low for 8 hours.
5. Allow contents to cool, then use a slotted spoon to place the solids (beef and veggies) into the bowl of a food processor. Process until lumps are gone, adding the liquid from the slow cooker 1 tablespoon at a time until a smooth, spoonable consistency is reached.
6. Use within 1 week or freeze for up to 6 months. To freeze small portions, use an ice cube tray or small silicone molds. Once frozen, cubes can be popped out of the tray/mold and stored in freezer bags or containers.

Slow-Cooked Chicken

High-quality chicken is actually much harder to find than high-quality beef. Ideally, chickens should be raised on pasture and if supplemental feed is necessary, it should be organic. The vast majority of grocery store chickens do not come close to these standards. If you have access to local pasture-raised chicken at a farmer's market or co-op, that would be a great option. If not, organic chicken is acceptable. It is unlikely that organic chickens were raised outdoors, but at least they will have received organic feed.

Ingredients
- 1 medium yellow onion, sliced
- 2 teaspoons garlic powder
- 1 teaspoon salt
- 1 teaspoon dried rosemary
- 1 teaspoon dried parsley
- 1/2 teaspoon black pepper
- 1 whole chicken, 3 to 5 pounds, giblets removed

Preparation
1. Scatter the onion slices in the bottom of a slow cooker.
2. In a small dish, combine the garlic powder, salt, rosemary, parsley and pepper. Rub the entire chicken with the seasoning mix.
3. Place the whole chicken, breast side down, on top of the onions.
4. Cook on high for 4 hours.
5. Allow contents to cool, then transfer the chicken to a cutting board. Use a carving knife or your hands to separate the meat and skin from the bones. Place the meat and skin into the bowl of a food processor. Use a slotted spoon to add the onions to the food processor

as well. Process until lumps are gone, adding the liquid from the slow cooker one tablespoon at a time until a smooth, spoonable consistency is reached.

6. Use within 1 week or freeze for up to 6 months. To freeze small portions, use an ice cube tray or small silicone molds. Once frozen, cubes can be popped out of the tray/mold and stored in freezer bags or containers.

CHICKEN LIVER PATE

For this recipe, any type of liver will work; however, chicken and beef liver are the most common. Chicken liver is much milder in flavor, though it is unlikely that baby will discriminate. As with the other meat recipes, animal quality is extremely important. Try to find liver from pasture-raised or grass-fed animals. If you don't want to take the plunge into cooking liver, you could also try any store-bought pâté, liverwurst or braunschweiger sausage with a simple and recognizable ingredient list.

Ingredients
- 1 pound liver, cut into 2-inch pieces
- 1 cup stock (beef, chicken, turkey or vegetable are all fine)
- 2 tablespoons unsalted butter
- 1/4 teaspoon salt

Preparation
1. Combine the liver, stock, butter and salt in a small saucepan. Bring to a boil, then lower the heat to a simmer. Simmer for 8 minutes.
2. Transfer the liver and the liquid to the bowl of a food processor. Pulse until creamy and spoonable.
3. Use within 1 week or freeze for up to 6 months. To freeze small portions, use an ice cube tray or small silicone molds. Once frozen, cubes can be popped out of the tray/mold and stored in freezer bags or containers.

FISH

Nearly everyone can benefit from increasing the amount of fish in their diet. The modern diet includes a disproportionate amount of omega-6 fatty acids found in processed seed oils such as corn oil, soybean oil and sunflower oil.[17] These fatty acids promote inflammation in the body and are largely accountable for the increasing number of inflammatory conditions seen today. On the contrary, fish contain anti-inflammatory omega-3 fatty acids. By increasing fish intake and making an effort to reduce the use of seed oils, we can help avoid excess inflammation in ourselves and our children.

From a palate standpoint, fish is one of the number one foods rejected by adults. Perhaps their families did not eat a lot of fish when they were growing up, or the fish they did eat was less than delicious. Starting your little ones early with seafood can prevent them from eliminating this critically nutritious food group from their diet later in life.

WHIPPED SALMON

This recipe takes advantage of canned salmon, which makes it perfect for sleep- and time-deprived parents! Try to find a brand that is wild-caught. Wild salmon have a much more nutritious diet than farmed salmon, and that impacts the nutrient content of the fish. And by all means, if you have access to fresh or frozen wild-caught salmon and would like to cook it from scratch, more power to you!

Ingredients
- 2 (6-ounce) cans of boneless salmon, packed in water, no salt added
- 1/4 cup plain, whole milk Greek yogurt
- 1 tablespoon unsalted butter, melted
- 1 teaspoon lemon juice
- 1/2 teaspoon dried dill
- 1/2 teaspoon salt
- Water, as needed

Preparation
1. Drain the salmon, then place it in the bowl of a food processor.
2. Add the yogurt, butter, lemon juice, dill and salt.
3. Process until lumps are gone, adding water 1 tablespoon at a time as needed until a smooth, spoonable consistency is reached.
4. Use within 1 week or freeze for up to 6 months. To freeze small portions, use an ice cube tray or small silicone molds. Once frozen, cubes can be popped out of the tray/mold and stored in freezer bags or containers.

BABY'S FIRST TUNA SALAD

This is the perfect way to prepare baby for a lifetime of tuna salad sandwiches in his/her lunchbox! It has all the familiar flavors of the popular sandwich, pureed for little mouths. Much like salmon, try to find wild-caught canned tuna for optimal nutrition.

Ingredients
- 3 (5-ounce) cans tuna, packed in water, no salt added
- 1/3 cup plain, whole milk Greek yogurt
- 1 celery stalk, sliced
- 1/4 of a large red onion, roughly chopped
- 1 teaspoon capers
- 1 teaspoon lemon juice
- 1/4 teaspoon salt
- 1/8 teaspoon black pepper
- Water, as needed

Preparation
1. Drain the tuna, then place it in the bowl of a food processor.
2. Add the yogurt, celery, red onion, capers, lemon juice, salt and pepper.
3. Process until lumps are gone, adding water, 1 tablespoon at a time, as needed until a smooth, spoonable consistency is reached.
4. Use within 1 week or freeze for up to 6 months. To freeze small portions, use an ice cube tray or small silicone molds. Once frozen, cubes can be popped out of the tray/mold and stored in freezer bags or containers.

FRUIT

Fruit is one of the most popular early foods, and for good reason. It is easy to find and prepare, and most babies enjoy the taste. However, there are a few tricks to helping your baby get the most out of fruits at this early age. First, we must take into account the pectin content. Pectin is a type of soluble fiber found in many types of fruit. Raw pectin can be irritating to the digestive tract, so only low-pectin fruits should be served raw.[18] Next, we need to remember that fruit does not contain any fat. Many of fruit's valuable nutrients can only be absorbed in the presence of fat, so it is important to make fruit purees that include a source of fat. And finally, purees are our chance to introduce babies to flavor, and fruit is no exception. Adding your family's favorite herbs and spices to your fruit purees is a great way to broaden the palate.

BABY GUACAMOLE

Avocado has quickly become a favorite first food. And while beef still tops my list thanks to its iron content, I can't argue against avocado's great qualities. Most obviously, there is the fact that it is one of the only fruits that contains fat! Babies are very well equipped to digest fat, and in turn fat is critical for their growth and development. All of the other fruit recipes in this book will require you to add a source of fat, but avocado can stand on its own! Instead, we can use it as a vehicle for flavor, mimicking a mild version of the ever-popular guacamole.

Ingredients
- 1 medium ripe avocado, halved and peeled
- 1 teaspoon cilantro, minced
- 1/2 teaspoon lime juice
- 1/8 teaspoon salt
- 1/8 teaspoon pepper

Preparation
1. Place all ingredients in the bowl of a small food processor. Pulse until lumps are gone. For older babies who can handle more lumps, this step can be done by hand with a fork or potato masher.
2. Serve right away, or within a day or two. If storing, transfer to a bowl and press plastic wrap around the puree, trying to avoid trapping any air between the food and the plastic. This will help slow browning.

Peanut Butter Bananas

Introducing peanuts early has been shown to reduce the risk for peanut allergy. However, their texture makes them a bit tricky to serve. They are a choking hazard in their whole form, and sticky peanut butter can be tough for babies to manipulate in their mouths. By pureeing a little peanut butter into bananas, babies learn a popular flavor combination while getting a dose of healthy fats with their fruit. It is also worth noting that bananas, especially less ripe green bananas, are a great antidote to occasional diarrhea.[19]

Ingredients
- 1 medium banana, sliced
- 2 tablespoons natural peanut butter (containing only peanuts and salt)

Preparation
1. Place the banana and peanut butter into the bowl of a small food processor. Pulse until lumps are gone and peanut butter is well combined with the banana. For older babies who can handle more lumps, this step can be done by hand with a fork or potato masher.
2. Serve right away, or within a day or two. If storing, transfer to a bowl and press plastic wrap around the puree, trying to avoid trapping any air between the food and the plastic. This will help slow browning.

TROPICAL BABY SORBET

Low-pectin tropical fruits such as mango and papaya are a great baby food option. Many stores now carry frozen varieties that make this recipe a snap. Be prepared to steal a few bites for yourself – it's probably the closest you'll get to a beach vacation for a while!

Ingredients
- 32 ounces frozen mango chunks, defrosted in the refrigerator at least 8 hours or overnight
- 2/3 cup coconut cream from a 13.5-ounce can of coconut milk (this is the thick, white, creamy part – you can discard the thin watery part or save it for another use)
- 1/4 teaspoon salt

Preparation
1. Place the defrosted mango chunks in the bowl of a food processor. Add the coconut cream and salt and pulse until smooth and creamy.
2. Use within 1 week or freeze for up to 6 months. To freeze small portions, use an ice cube tray or small silicone molds. Once frozen, cubes can be popped out of the tray/mold and stored in freezer bags or containers.

PEACHES & CREAM

This classic combination will have baby begging for more! Fresh peaches can be tough to find out of season, so this recipe takes advantage of canned peaches. Be sure to look for them in 100% fruit juice rather than syrup or light syrup. Peaches are sweet enough on their own, so there is no need to add sugar to them. Note that this puree turns out pretty thin. If you would like it thicker, consider stirring it into some plain, whole milk Greek yogurt just before serving.

Ingredients
- 3 (15-ounce) cans peaches in 100% juice, drained and rinsed with cold water, or 5 cups peeled, sliced fresh peaches
- 1/2 cup heavy whipping cream
- 1 teaspoon lemon juice
- 1/8 teaspoon cinnamon
- 1/8 teaspoon nutmeg

Preparation
1. Place peaches in a medium saucepan. Cook over medium heat for 10 to 15 minutes, stirring often. Peaches are done cooking once they start to fall apart and can be easily smashed with a wooden spoon.
2. Transfer peaches and their liquid to the bowl of a food processor. Add lemon juice, cream, cinnamon and nutmeg. Pulse until smooth.
3. Use within 1 week or freeze for up to 6 months. To freeze small portions, use an ice cube tray or small silicone molds. Once frozen, cubes can be popped out of the tray/mold and stored in freezer bags or containers.

MIXED BERRY FRO-YO

Fresh berries can be expensive, especially out of season, but frozen are easy to come by and still have great flavor. A bag of frozen mixed berries is the perfect way to introduce your little one to these antioxidant-rich gems. Note that this puree turns out pretty thin. If you would like it thicker, consider stirring it into applesauce or adding extra plain, whole milk Greek yogurt just before serving.

Ingredients
- 20 ounces frozen mixed berries, defrosted in the refrigerator at least 8 hours or overnight
- 1 teaspoon lemon juice
- 1 cup plain, whole milk Greek yogurt

Preparation
1. Place berries in a small saucepan. Cook over medium heat for about 5 minutes, stirring often. Berries are done cooking once they start to fall apart and can be easily smashed with a wooden spoon.
2. Transfer berries and their liquid to the bowl of a food processor. Add lemon juice and yogurt. Pulse until smooth.
3. Use within 1 week or freeze for up to 6 months. To freeze small portions, use an ice cube tray or small silicone molds. Once frozen, cubes can be popped out of the tray/mold and stored in freezer bags or containers.

SLOW COOKER APPLESAUCE

Confession: we used only store-bought apple sauce with our oldest child. I made 90% of her baby food, but sometimes I needed to cut corners for my own sanity. Much to my delight, a number of brands make organic applesauce without any added sugar or weird ingredients. And since it is not technically baby food, you don't pay the insane markup you will see on those little jars. But when our second child turned six months in the fall, I just couldn't pass up the farmer's market bounty of fresh, local apples. In retrospect, I think he was the big winner, as the flavor of homemade applesauce is far superior to store-bought!

Ingredients
- 3 pounds apples, peeled and cut into 1-inch cubes (you should get about 16 cubes per apple)
- 1/2 cup water
- 4 tablespoons unsalted butter, cut into 4 pieces
- 2 cinnamon sticks
- 1 tablespoon lemon juice
- 1/4 teaspoon salt

Preparation
1. Place all ingredients in a slow cooker.
2. Cook on high for 3 hours.
3. Remove the cinnamon sticks.
4. Transfer apple mixture into the bowl of a food processor and pulse until smooth.
5. Use within 1 week or freeze for up to 6 months. To freeze small portions, use an ice cube tray or small silicone molds. Once frozen, cubes can be popped out of the tray/mold and stored in freezer bags or containers.

PRUNE PUREE

The fruit section would not be complete without the ultimate constipation tonic: prune puree.[20] Many babies will go through bouts of constipation from time to time as their gut adjusts to solid foods. Having some prune puree on hand is a great way to nip any issues in the bud without resorting to juice or medication. That being said, if your little one tends toward looser stools or is dealing with any diarrhea, this is *not* the puree for you!

Ingredients
- 12 prunes
- Boiling water to cover
- 1 tablespoon olive oil

Preparation
1. Place the prunes in a heat-proof bowl. Pour boiling water over the prunes until they are completely submerged. Allow to stand for 20 minutes.
2. Use tongs or a slotted spoon to remove prunes from soaking water and transfer to the bowl of a food processor. Add olive oil. Process until smooth, adding the warm soaking water slowly as needed to create a smooth puree.
3. Use within 1 week or freeze for up to 6 months. To freeze small portions, use an ice cube tray or small silicone molds. Once frozen, cubes can be popped out of the tray/mold and stored in freezer bags or containers.

VEGETABLES

Vegetables should taste good. I will say it again for good measure: vegetables should taste *good*! I have spent many years working with adults who choke down plain, steamed veggies in the name of health, but when pressed will admit that they "don't like vegetables." That is because vegetables need three key elements to taste delicious: seasoning, fat and heat. Plain, steamed squash bears little resemblance to one that was roasted with butter and pureed with herbs, acid and walnuts. Your little darling deserves to know good vegetables from the start, so step away from the flavorless jars and whip up something your baby will enjoy for the rest of his/her life.

* *

ROASTED SQUASH PUREE
Whenever I have the misfortune of eating plain, steamed winter squash, all I can think of is baby food. Ironically, my goal for this recipe was to create a puree that tastes nothing like that! Roasting the squash instead of steaming or boiling brings out its nutty flavor, and adding walnuts, sage and balsamic vinegar ensures that this puree will please kids and adults alike! I used acorn squash, but any winter squash such as pumpkin or butternut can be substituted.

Ingredients
- 2 acorn squash, about 3 to 4 pounds total
- 2 tablespoons unsalted butter, divided

- 1/4 teaspoon salt
- 1/3 cup walnuts, chopped
- 1 tablespoon balsamic vinegar
- 1/2 teaspoon dried sage

Preparation
1. Preheat oven to 425°F.
2. Slice off the stem end of one squash. Stand it up on the now-flat top and slice it down the center. Use a spoon to scoop out the seeds. Repeat with the second squash.
3. Place squash halves, cut side up, on a baking sheet. If desired, you can line the baking sheet with foil for easier cleanup.
4. Melt 1 tablespoon of butter. Use a pastry brush to brush the melted butter onto the flesh of each squash. Cut the remaining tablespoon of butter into 4 pieces. Drop one piece into the hollow well of each squash. Sprinkle evenly with salt.
5. Bake for 50 minutes. Remove from the oven and set aside until cool enough to handle.
6. Use a spoon to scrape the flesh from each squash into the bowl of a food processor. Add the walnuts, balsamic vinegar and sage. Process until lumps are gone, taking care to make certain that the walnut pieces are completely pureed.
7. Use within 1 week or freeze for up to 6 months. To freeze small portions, use an ice cube tray or small silicone molds. Once frozen, cubes can be popped out of the tray/mold and stored in freezer bags or containers.

MASHED SWEET POTATOES

I couldn't leave out this classic baby food favorite. Of course, in my version, there is ample fat and a dash of "adult" spices to ensure that the result is both nourishing and palate-building. And since mashed sweet potatoes are a perfectly acceptable side dish for any meal, you can serve the whole family with this one!

Ingredients
- 1 to 2 pounds sweet potatoes
- 4 tablespoons unsalted butter, melted
- 2 tablespoons whole milk, plus more as needed
- 1/4 teaspoon salt
- 1/8 teaspoon cinnamon
- 1/8 teaspoon nutmeg

Preparation
1. Preheat oven to 400°F.
2. Poke the potatoes with a fork, at least 5 or 6 pokes per potato. Place the potatoes on a baking sheet. If desired, you can line the baking sheet with foil for easier cleanup. Bake for 1 hour, until very tender. Allow to cool.
3. Gently peel the skins off the potatoes and place the flesh into the bowl of a food processor. Add melted butter, milk, salt, cinnamon and nutmeg. Puree until smooth and creamy, adding more milk as needed.
4. Use within 1 week or freeze for up to 6 months. To freeze small portions, use an ice cube tray or small silicone molds. Once frozen, cubes can be popped out of the tray/mold and stored in freezer bags or containers.

GARLIC AND HERB MASHED POTATOES

Mashed potatoes are the perfect chance to introduce baby to everyone's favorite flavoring agent: garlic! It is never too early to start with bold flavors, and potatoes are a great vehicle for a variety of herbs and spices. As with the previous sweet potato recipe, you will probably have the whole family begging for a taste!

Ingredients
- 1 1/2 pounds Yukon gold potatoes, peeled and cut into 2-inch cubes
- 4 ounces garlic and herb goat cheese
- 4 tablespoons unsalted butter, melted
- 1/4 cup milk, plus more as needed
- 1/2 teaspoon kosher salt

Preparation
1. Place the cubed potatoes in a large pot and cover completely with water. Bring to a boil over high heat, then reduce heat to maintain a simmer. Simmer 20 to 25 minutes, or until potatoes can easily be pierced with a fork. Drain and allow to cool slightly.
2. Place potatoes, goat cheese, melted butter, milk and salt into the bowl of a food processor. Process until smooth and creamy, adding more milk as needed. If baby can handle a few lumps, this step can also be done in the pot with a potato masher.
3. Use within 1 week or freeze for up to 6 months. To freeze small portions, use an ice cube tray or small silicone molds. Once frozen, cubes can be popped out of the tray/mold and stored in freezer bags or containers.

Yogurt Parfaits

Plain, whole milk yogurt is a miracle food. First and foremost, babies love it. Why companies insist on marketing sweetened, flavored yogurts to babies and kids I will never know, because plain yogurt in all its tart glory is the thing baby dreams are made of. Kids do NOT require flavored yogurt. Period. Never. That being said, yogurt "parfaits" can be a lifesaver in a busy household. If your baby seems at all hesitant about a new puree, simply stir it into some plain, whole milk yogurt and viola, baby heaven. Yogurt can easily transition from sweet to savory, so you can mix it with fruit purees, meat purees and even with a mashed version of whatever you ate for dinner the night before. You can also use it to thicken soups or take the edge off of anything slightly spicy.

Greek yogurt is a little thicker than traditional, so it tends to work better for these applications, but either type is packed with probiotics, vitamins and minerals. The most important thing is that you look for varieties marked "plain" and "whole milk." It is often hard to find this combination in the smaller containers, but most stores sell it in the larger tubs.

FINGER FOODS (9+ MONTHS)

Something magical happens around nine months: babies develop the pincer grasp. This is the ability to pick up small objects using the thumb and forefinger. Until this milestone, babies will only be able to pick up foods shaped like long strips, which they grip in their fist like a bat. Some parents feel comfortable letting babies gnaw on large strips of food, but many are wary of the potential for choking. And while purees are a great way to introduce flavors, they are a ton of work! Not only do you have to make them, but you also have to spoon-feed them. The arrival of the pincer grasp means that baby can start to join the family table, feeding him/herself while everyone else eats.

Ultimately the goal is for baby to simply eat a cut-up version of your nutritious and delicious family meal. But at first you may find it handy to use foods that lend themselves easily to small pieces.

PACKAGED FINGER FOOD

In the puree section, I gave you the go-ahead to purchase store-bought purees if desired. For the most part, that allowance ends here. Once your child can handle finger foods, there is absolutely no reason to purchase foods marketed toward babies or kids. Companies charge an exorbitant amount for high-carbohydrate, poorly seasoned, overly packaged foods, knowing that well-intentioned but ultimately unknowledgeable parents will happily shell out the cash. Meanwhile, the healthiest and tastiest foods for growing babies are just cut-up versions of the exact same foods you should be eating!

One of the most common questions I receive is related to "puffs" or Cheerios as a mess-free way for babies to practice the pincer grasp. I can say with confidence that every human in history managed to figure out the pincer grasp despite Cheerios' arrival on the scene in 1940 and "puffs" as recently as the 21st century. Real-food alternatives include dehydrated fruit, small pieces of shredded meat, slivered almonds, beans, small pieces of cheese and cut-up hard-boiled eggs, to name a few. Babies do not need snacks, only meals and milk, so the fact that these foods are less portable should not be a big issue. For sample eating schedules at all ages, refer to the Quick Guide at the beginning of this book.

MEAT

Meat continues to be a great option for expanding baby's palate and providing nutrients that are not available in breast milk or formula. Of course, certain meats present a texture problem for a mostly toothless nine-month-old, so special care should be taken to choose things that are easy to gum. Poultry, especially slow-cooked poultry, is very moist and tender and can be torn into small, easy-to-grasp pieces. Red meat can be tougher, so starting with ground meat makes life easier for everyone.

* *

BEEF AND PORK MEATBALLS

Meatballs are a simple way to serve ground meat to little hands. They are easy to pick up but come apart readily even in a toothless mouth. Plus they are great for the whole family to enjoy, and they freeze well when you need something quick for baby.

Ingredients

- 2 eggs
- 3/4 cup almond flour
- 1/2 cup whole milk
- 1 pound ground beef
- 1 pound ground pork
- 2 teaspoons Italian seasoning
- 2 teaspoons kosher salt
- 1 teaspoon garlic powder
- 1 teaspoon pepper
- Non-stick spray

Preparation

1. Preheat oven to 400°F.
2. Crack the eggs into a large bowl and whisk to break them up.
3. Add the almond flour and whole milk and whisk to combine.
4. Add the beef, pork, Italian seasoning, salt, garlic powder and pepper. Use your hands to mix everything together, but do not over-mix.
5. Spray a baking sheet with non-stick spray or brush with olive oil. If desired, you can line the baking sheet with foil for easier cleanup. Form the mixture into about 20 golf-ball-sized meatballs. Space the meatballs evenly on the baking sheet. Bake for 25 to 30 minutes, until their internal temperature registers 165°F on a meat thermometer and they are no longer pink inside.
6. For babies who have mastered the pincer grasp, you can break the meatballs into smaller pieces. For younger babies without the pincer grasp, serve whole or cut into quarters.

Slow-Cooked Chicken

Slow cookers are a busy family's best friend. Hands-off cooking at its finest, this method allows you to prepare tender, nutritious and delicious meat while you are off playing with your little one (or, let's be honest, doing more laundry).

Ingredients
- 1 medium onion, sliced
- 2 teaspoons Italian seasoning
- 2 teaspoons paprika
- 1 teaspoon kosher salt
- 1 whole chicken

Preparation
1. Arrange the onion slices on the bottom of a slow cooker.
2. Mix the Italian seasoning, paprika and salt in a small bowl. Rub over the entire chicken.
3. Place the seasoned chicken on top of the onion slices, breast side down.
4. Cook on high for 5 hours.
5. Transfer the chicken to a cutting board and shred, separating the meat from the skin and bones. For babies who have mastered the pincer grasp, chop the meat into small, fingernail-sized pieces. For younger babies without the pincer grasp, shred it into long strips.

FISH

No special recipe is needed to prepare fish for babies. It is naturally flaky, soft and easy to pick up, making it the perfect finger food. You can bake or pan-fry fresh or frozen fish, or serve canned seafood such as tuna, salmon or sardines. You will want to double check that all bones have been removed to avoid a choking hazard. You can also offer shellfish such as shrimp or crab. The only thing to avoid is breaded, deep-fried fish – no fish sticks necessary for your healthy little foodie!

VEGETABLES

Vegetables taste amazing when they are cooked in a little fat and salt. It brings out their natural sweetness and creates a much more interesting texture. They also provide a chance to incorporate herbs and spices to prepare baby's palate for family meals. As an added bonus, long, skinny vegetables are easy for babies to eat, even if their pincer grasp is not perfect yet.

SLOW-COOKED CARROTS

Carrots are a home-run veggie in our house. Cooking really brings out their sweetness, and perhaps because we don't offer a ton of fruit, carrots seem downright decadent when it comes to side dishes. Any type of carrot works well for this recipe, although baby carrots allow you skip all that pesky chopping.

Ingredients
- 1 pound baby carrots, or larger carrots cut into finger-sized strips
- 1/3 cup apple juice
- 2 tablespoons butter, cut into 8 pieces
- 1/4 teaspoon salt

Preparation
1. Place the carrots in a medium or small slow cooker. Pour in the apple juice. Sprinkle with salt, then dot with the butter.
2. Cook on high for about 4 hours, stirring every 1 to 2 hours, until carrots are fork-tender.
3. Cool slightly, then serve as-is and allow baby to gnaw on the carrot sticks, or cut into small pieces if baby's pincer grasp is well developed.

Roasted Broccoli

When broccoli is roasted in fat, the florets caramelize, giving them a faintly potato chip-esque flavor. And while of course we don't want babies addicted to potato chips, getting them addicted to broccoli might be a good thing! If you do not have coconut oil on hand, you can substitute olive oil or butter, but for some reason the flavor is just a notch better with the coconut oil.

Ingredients
- 3 cups broccoli, cut into florets with an inch or so of stem till attached for easier grasping
- 2 tablespoon coconut oil, melted
- 1/2 teaspoon garlic powder
- 1/4 teaspoon kosher salt

Preparation
1. Preheat oven to 400°F.
2. Place broccoli in a large bowl and toss with melted coconut oil, garlic powder and salt.
3. Transfer the broccoli to a baking sheet and arrange it evenly in a single layer. If desired, you can line the baking sheet with foil for easier cleanup.
4. Bake for 15 minutes.
5. Cool slightly, then serve as long stalks that baby can gnaw on or cut into small pieces if baby's pincer grasp is well developed.

Sautéed Green Beans

I am pretty sure my daughter ate her weight in green beans at her first Thanksgiving. She was 11 months old at the time and pretty much the whole family sat there stunned as she shoved one bean after another into her mouth in pure ecstasy. Older babies are weird like that – they go through phases where they are obsessed with one particular food for a few weeks and then poof, they move on to something else. Nonetheless, I think green beans, especially when sautéed in butter and topped with salt, are a pretty big hit with most babies.

Ingredients
- 1 pound green beans, ends trimmed
- 3 tablespoons unsalted butter
- 1 tablespoon garlic, minced
- 1/2 teaspoon salt

Preparation
1. Place the green beans in an even layer on a microwave-safe plate. Cover them with three layers of damp paper towels or one clean, damp kitchen towel. Microwave on high for six minutes. Set aside. If you prefer to avoid using a microwave, you can instead bring a large pot of water to a boil, then add the green beans and cook for 4 minutes before draining and setting aside.
2. Melt butter in a large skillet over medium heat. Add the garlic and cook, stirring, until fragrant, about 30 seconds.
3. Add the green beans, toss to coat in the butter, and sauté, stirring occasionally, for 5 minutes.
4. Add salt, tossing to combine.

5. Cool slightly, then serve as-is and allow baby to gnaw on the whole beans, or cut into small pieces if baby's pincer grasp is well developed.

* *

ROASTED RED PEPPER STRIPS

Red bell peppers pack in twice as much vitamin C per cup than oranges, but with much less sugar and many more culinary uses. Introducing this flavor to babies at a young age sets them up to enjoy countless recipes, not to mention the option of using peppers as dip-scoopers instead of less nutritious chips or crackers.

Ingredients
- 2 medium bell peppers
- 1 tablespoon olive oil
- 1/4 teaspoon salt

Preparation
1. Preheat the oven to 450°F.
2. Remove the stems and seeds from the peppers, then cut the flesh into finger-sized strips.
3. Place the pepper strips in a bowl and toss with olive oil and salt.
4. Spread the strips out on a baking sheet. If desired, you can line the baking sheet with foil for easier cleanup. Bake for 15–20 minutes, until softened.
5. Cool slightly, then serve as-is and allow baby to gnaw on the strips, or cut into small pieces if baby's pincer grasp is well developed.

BROILED ASPARAGUS

Asparagus is the perfect shape for young hands, but the skin can be a little tough to gum through. Peeling the stalks will remove the overly fibrous outer layer and allow little mouths to enjoy this delicious spring vegetable.

Ingredients
- 1 pound asparagus, bottom 2 inches trimmed
- 2 tablespoon olive oil
- 1/4 teaspoon kosher salt
- 1/8 teaspoon pepper

Preparation
1. Place an oven rack 2 inches below the heat element and preheat the oven to broil.
2. Use a vegetable peeler to peel the lower half of each asparagus spear. This is easiest if you lay the asparagus on a cutting board and rotate it until all sides are peeled.
3. Arrange the asparagus in a single layer on a baking sheet. If desired, you can line the baking sheet with foil for easier cleanup. Drizzle with the oil, then sprinkle with salt and pepper.
4. Broil until tender and starting to brown, 6 to 8 minutes.
5. Cool slightly, then serve as-is and allow baby to gnaw on the stalks, or cut into small pieces if baby's pincer grasp is well developed.

FRUIT

Fruit is a popular option thanks to its availability, portable nature and general acceptance by most babies. However, I typically do not recommend going overboard in the fruit category as it can set baby up to prefer sweet foods. Try not to offer it more than once or twice a day and utilize a wide variety of fruits to expand baby's palate.

To prepare raw fruit for babies, peel first, then cut into small pieces – about the size of your pinky nail is a good reference. Ripe apples and pears are a good place to start because their texture makes them easy for babies to pick up, but you can also try other fruits, including bananas, berries, mandarin oranges and tropical fruits such as mango or papaya.

EGGS

Eggs are a phenomenal finger food for babies. They are generally well liked, super easy to make and contain lots of fat and protein for your growing child. Scrambled eggs are very easy for baby to pick up and eat, as are chopped hard-boiled eggs.

Scrambled Eggs

There is no faster protein than scrambled eggs, and they are not limited to breakfast – eggs are perfect for any meal when you are in a hurry and have a hungry baby on your hands.

Ingredients
- 2 eggs
- 2 tablespoons whole milk
- 1/8 teaspoon kosher salt
- 1/8 teaspoon pepper
- 1 tablespoon unsalted butter

Preparation
1. Crack the eggs into a bowl. Add the milk, salt and pepper. Whisk for at least 10 to 20 seconds, until foamy.
2. Melt butter in a small sauté pan over medium-low heat. Add eggs.
3. Cook eggs, stirring gently but constantly until all moisture is gone and eggs are fully cooked. Transfer to a dish and let cool slightly.
4. For babies who have mastered the pincer grasp, break the eggs into small, fingernail-sized pieces. For younger babies without the pincer grasp, cut into long, finger-shaped strips. Before serving, make sure the eggs are not too hot to the touch.

Hard-Boiled Eggs

Hard-boiled eggs are the ultimate make-ahead option for busy families. After boiling, eggs can be stored in their shells for up to a week in the refrigerator, giving you lots of options for quick and easy meals. Be sure to offer the whole egg, as the yolks and whites have different and complementary nutrition.

Ingredients
- 2 eggs
- 1/8 teaspoon kosher salt
- 1/8 teaspoon pepper

Preparation
1. Fill a small pot with enough water to submerge two eggs (but don't put the eggs in yet). Bring to a boil.
2. Use tongs to gently place each egg into the pot.
3. Allow to boil for 30 seconds.
4. Cover the pot and reduce heat to low. Simmer for 11 minutes.
5. Transfer eggs to a bowl of ice water and let sit for at least 5 minutes.
6. To serve immediately, peel and cut into quarters or eighths. Sprinkle the pieces with salt and pepper.
7. To serve later, leave shells on and store in the fridge. Peel and season when ready to eat.

CHEESE

Like all sane humans, kids love cheese. This is great for
parents because good quality cheese is not only convenient,
but also high in essential proteins and fat. Try to introduce
kids to a wide variety of cheeses to build their palate. You
might be surprised at how many babies will happily scarf
down a musky bleu or tangy goat cheese if given the chance!
Of course, in a bind, a full-fat string cheese or cheese wheels
will also do the trick. Avoid highly processed American
cheeses, but everything else is fair game. Simply break or cut
the cheese into bite-sized pieces and watch your baby chow
down with delight!

NUTS

Nuts are one of the most overlooked finger food options.
While big-box brands are raking in money with highly
processed "puffs" and other man-made finger foods, the
humble nut is stuck in the back of pantries begging to be set
free! Of course, many nuts present choking hazards if not
prepared properly. One of my favorite safe options is slivered
almonds. Easy and delicious, they are already cut into the
perfect shape for tiny fingers and mouths. Chopped walnuts

and pecans are also great, as their softer texture is easy to gum. Since they do not need refrigeration, nuts are perfect to toss in your bag for meals on the go. Ground fruit and nut bars such as Larabar can also be a good addition to your meals from time to time.

BEANS

Beans are literally nature's finger food. Small, soft varieties such as black beans are tailor-made for babies practicing their pincer grasp. If you are concerned about choking or want to serve larger varieties such as kidney beans, simply smash the beans up a bit before serving.

Canned beans are a great option for quick and easy meals. Try to buy varieties with no added ingredients and packed in BPA-free cans. Always rinse and drain the beans before serving. Even better, soak and cook dried beans at home. The preparation is fairly hands-off thanks to the handy slow cooker, and the finished beans can be frozen for quicker use in the future.

BLACK BEANS

Black beans cook up nice and soft, making them perfect for babies who are still a bit teeth-challenged! And a baby who likes black beans is great to dine out with down the road since many cuisines offer them as a soup or side dish.

Ingredients
- 1 pound dried black beans
- 1 tablespoon plus 1 teaspoon kosher salt, divided

Preparation
1. Sort through the beans to ensure there are no rocks or debris. Place the beans in a large bowl or pot. Sprinkle with 1 tablespoon of salt, then fill the bowl with enough water to cover the beans by at least 2 inches. Cover with a towel and set aside. Allow the beans to soak for 8 hours or overnight.
2. Drain the beans in a large colander, rinsing with cold water to remove any excess salt.
3. Transfer the beans to your slow cooker and sprinkle with the remaining teaspoon of salt. Fill the slow cooker with enough water to cover the beans by about 2 inches. Cook on low for 5 hours, or until soft and creamy.
4. Drain the beans in a large colander and allow them to cool.
5. Serve as is, or smashed slightly to make them easier to pick up.
6. Use within 1 week or freeze for up to 6 months. To freeze, line a baking sheet with parchment paper, then spread the beans out on the sheet. Cover with plastic wrap and place in the freezer overnight, or until beans are frozen solid. Transfer the beans to a gallon bag or other storage container.

CHICKPEAS

Chickpeas, also known as garbanzo beans, are a great bean to get kids used to since hummus is a nice food to keep in the repertoire down the road. Smashing them up just a bit makes them easier to pick up and chew.

Ingredients
- 1 pound dried chickpeas
- 1 tablespoon plus 1 teaspoon kosher salt, divided

Preparation
1. Sort through the beans to ensure there are no rocks or debris. Place the beans in a large bowl or pot. Sprinkle with 1 tablespoon of salt, then fill the bowl with enough water to cover the beans by at least 2 inches. Cover with a towel and set aside. Allow the beans to soak for 8 hours or overnight.
2. Drain the beans in a large colander, rinsing with cold water to remove any excess salt.
3. Transfer the beans to your slow cooker and sprinkle with the remaining teaspoon of salt. Fill the slow cooker with enough water to cover the beans by about 2 inches. Cook on low for 5 hours, or until soft and tender.
4. Drain the beans in a large colander and allow them to cool.
5. Serve as is, or smashed slightly to make them easier to pick up.
6. Use within 1 week or freeze for up to 6 months. To freeze, line a baking sheet with parchment paper, then spread the beans out on the sheet. Cover with plastic wrap and place in the freezer overnight, or until beans are frozen solid. Transfer the beans to a gallon bag or other storage container.

WHOLE GRAINS

Grains, namely wheat, rice, oats and corn, are perhaps the most over-eaten foods in the American diet. Despite playing a relatively small role in the historical human diet, today more than 50% of world daily caloric intake comes from grains.[21] Unfortunately most of those grains are heavily refined and nearly devoid of nutrition beyond carbohydrate calories. It is very easy to fall into the trap of feeding kids refined grains at every meal simply because they tend to like them. I challenge parents to break this cycle by limiting the number of meals at which they offer grain foods. Including brown rice, oats, corn or 100% whole grain products such as bread, pasta or crackers is fine at one or two meals a day. But you will likely notice that if you offer large portions of these foods your child will decide not to eat anything else on their plate. At the very least, try to commingle whole grain foods with other, more nutritious elements. Below are some excellent ways to incorporate whole grains into your meals.

- Whole wheat pasta topped with homemade sauce such as marinara, bolognaise, Alfredo or browned butter.
- Whole or sprouted grain bread topped with butter or peanut butter.

- Whole or sprouted grain bread or corn tortillas soaked in soup.

- Steel-cut or rolled oatmeal made with whole milk and sprinkled with fresh berries and crushed nuts.

- Brown rice stir-fried with vegetables, soy sauce and chicken or shrimp.

- Fresh or frozen corn topped with melted butter.

Perhaps most importantly, avoid the pitfalls of boxed cereal. Yes, it makes for easy finger food. But it is sweet, highly processed, devoid of nutrition and sure to become your baby's favorite food if given the chance. If you can find a puffed corn or puffed rice with no added ingredients, such as the ones by Arrowhead Mills, you can use that on a limited basis to practice the pincer grasp.

FAMILY FOOD

As your little one masters the pincer grasp, a beautiful thing starts to happen – he/she can eat the same things you are eating! Sometime between nine and twelve months, you will want to consider rearranging your family's meal schedule to allow your baby to join you as often as possible. Children are great mimics, and just watching you eat will encourage them to try new foods. Pull their high chair as close to the table as you can or consider a high chair that allows them to eat directly off the table. Try to serve them the same items that you are eating, modifying foods as needed for small mouths and fingers. Start to move away from spoon-feeding and allow baby to self-feed as much as possible. If the family dinner is soup, you can strain out the solid parts to offer on a plate, or soak whole or sprouted grain bread or tortillas in the broth for baby to enjoy. There are no off-limits foods at this point, other than honey due to its risk of transmitting botulinum spores. However, hyper-palatable processed foods containing sugar and/or refined grains will quickly become a child's favorite if offered frequently. In order to avoid these non-nutritious foods displacing nourishing whole foods, do not make them available on a regular basis. You will also want to go easy on spicy foods made with hot peppers. If this is a big part of your family's diet, start very small to gauge your baby's tolerance.

Remember, breast milk and/or formula still provides the majority of your baby's calories at this stage. Do not feel concerned if the majority of a meal ends up on the floor or in the dog's mouth. The goal of food at this stage is to introduce flavor and allow baby to practice fine motor skills. You should see a marked increase in consumption between nine and twelve months, but it will not happen overnight. And whatever you do, avoid categorizing a food as something your baby "does not like." Babies choose to eat or not eat at any given moment based on a myriad of mysterious reasons. If you remove a food from your family's repertoire every time baby rejects it, you will be down to just bread and applesauce before baby turns one!

BEVERAGES

Breast milk or formula should still be the primary beverage from nine months until baby's first birthday. However, around 11 months, you may want to start offering a cup of water at meals. This will prepare baby to transition away from bottles around his/her first birthday. Speech and occupational therapists recommend straw-based cups or open cups as opposed to traditional sippy cups or prolonged bottle usage.[22] Bottles and sippy cups promote a more infantile suckling action, which children should be transitioning away from around 12 months old. Straw and open cups allow for a more "adult" tongue motion, helping with speech development as well as chewing and swallowing.

THE FAMILY TABLE (12+ MONTHS)

Happy birthday to your little foodie! And congratulations to you for navigating the most complex and ever-changing stages of feeding. You are now in the home stretch and can focus on creating a healthy little foodie whom you will enjoy dining with for years to come. At this point, your child should be able to eat "adult food" for every meal. While you will still need to cut things up for a while to come, there is typically no need to modify textures, spoon-feed or generally treat your little one like a baby. Welcome to the adult table, kiddo – you made it!

WEANING AND BEVERAGES

From a purely nutritional perspective, breast milk and formula are no longer necessary after 12 months. Toddlers should be getting all the vitamins and minerals that they need from food. If you are still nursing, you may choose to continue for other reasons, such as mother-baby bonding and improved immunity. However, you will want to structure the timing of your nursing schedule so as not to interfere with the child's hunger for solid foods. Below are some transition options, based on what you were doing before baby turned one. Note that bottles are not recommended beyond 12 months. Straw-based cups or open cups are better for oral muscle development and should replace bottles completely around baby's first birthday. Feel free to start out by mixing cow's milk with expressed breast milk or formula for a few days to get baby used to the taste.

Scenario 1: You were nursing baby after waking in the morning, after naps and before bed, for a total of four nursing sessions per day. You would like to continue nursing.
Transition Strategy: Nurse at morning wake, then after lunch and before bed. If you want to reduce nursing sessions as baby gets older, eliminate one session at a time, waiting at least a week before eliminating another. As you eliminate nursing sessions, offer expressed breast milk or whole cow's milk in a straw-based cup or open cup at the nearest meal instead. Around 15 months, you can offer water at meals instead of milk, if desired.

Scenario 2: You were nursing baby after waking in the morning, after naps and before bed, for a total of four nursing sessions per day. You would like to stop nursing. **Transition Strategy**: Start by nursing at morning wake, then after lunch and before bed. After a week or two, eliminate the lunch nursing session and offer expressed breast milk or whole cow's milk in a straw-based cup or open cup at lunch instead. After another week or two, eliminate either the morning nursing session or the bedtime nursing session and offer milk at the nearest meal instead. Finally, after another week or two, eliminate the remaining nursing session and offer milk at the nearest meal instead. Around 15 months, you can offer water at meals instead of milk, if desired.

Scenario 3: You were offering bottles of expressed breast milk or formula at morning wake, after naps and before bed, for a total of four bottles per day. **Transition Strategy**: Offer expressed breast milk or whole cow's milk in a straw-based cup or open cup instead of a bottle at all the times you were giving bottles – morning wake, after naps and before bed. After a few weeks, stop offering milk after naps and instead offer it at lunch. After a few more weeks, eliminate the feeding at morning wake and offer milk at breakfast instead. Finally, eliminate the bedtime feeding and offer milk at dinner instead. Around 15 months, you can offer water at meals instead of milk, if desired.

As your one-year-old ages, he/she will no longer need milk of any kind. Whole cow's milk does provide some nice nutrition and can be helpful in transitioning a child from liquid nourishment to solid nourishment, but it is by no means required. Around 15 months, consider offering water at two meals per day and milk at just one. You may opt to stop offering milk altogether, for a variety of reasons.[23,24]

One compelling reason to avoid or limit milk is if your child appears to be a picky eater. While there are certainly clinical reasons for picky eating, often it is simply a result of a child being full from milk and/or snacks. If your child appears disinterested in the food you are serving but consistently downs four or more ounces of milk at each meal, consider discontinuing milk or limiting it to a small serving at just one meal per day.

Another common issue is constipation due to high cow's milk intake.[25] If your child appears bloated, is not having as many bowel movements as before, is straining to poop or has very hard, dry feces, consider reducing or eliminating milk from the diet.

If you decide to reduce or eliminate cow's milk for the above reasons, or due to an intolerance or allergy, do not feel that you must provide a man-made "milk alternative." The juice squeezed from a nut, bean or seed does not nutritionally resemble the milk from a mammal's breast in any way. Manufacturers fortify these plant "milks" to better imitate cow's milk, but in that case you may as well just feed your toddler a multivitamin. Better yet, offer foods that contain the nutrients that would have been available in milk. A half teaspoon of NutraPro cod liver oil contains 2.5 times more vitamin D than a cup of milk, and calcium is plentiful in foods like kale, sardines and broccoli.

It goes without saying that soda, sports drinks and other sweetened beverages have no place in a child's diet (or anyone's, for that matter!). I urge parents to avoid them at all costs. A stickier issue is juice. Many pediatricians still give 100% juice the go-ahead on the basis that it contains some vitamins and minerals and does not have added sugar. I wholeheartedly disagree. There is no nutrient in juice that cannot be found in whole fruit or vegetables. Juice contains all of fruit's sugar and none of its fiber and it sets children up to love sweet flavors. It is essentially a gateway drug to preferring sweet beverages. In my adult practice, I frequently encounter patients who tell me they "do not like the taste of water." This is a travesty. Water is nature's beverage and the only one a human needs beyond infancy. A dislike of water must be learned, and that education starts with an innocent box of apple juice.

With regard to water intake, there is no minimum or maximum. It should be offered at all meals, and upon request between meals. As long as other, more addicting, beverages are not being offered, kids will drink the "right" amount of water naturally.

MEAL TIMING AND SNACKS

Hopefully you have begun to transition your little one to standard mealtimes over the past few months. If not, now is the time to get him/her used to a regular eating schedule of breakfast, lunch and dinner. If you are still nursing, try to restrict it to three times a day, just after meals. Do not offer milk between meals. The goal is to transition your child to solid food as the primary source of nutrition and the key to success is a child who shows up to the table hungry. Depending on your family's schedule, there may be a larger gap between two of your meals. You might consider adding a snack if your child seems particularly hungry during that gap. However, snacking should be done with great caution. Along with excess milk consumption, snacks are a key cause of "picky eating." Not only do they physically fill kids up close to meal time, but the majority of packaged snack foods are far more palatable than the fresh, whole foods served at meals. For this reason, I recommend a few key guidelines for snacking.

1. Serve foods that are nutrient dense and no more delicious than typical meal foods. Hard-boiled eggs, vegetables with hummus, string cheese, plain yogurt, celery with peanut butter and unsalted mixed nuts are great examples. Most kids will only eat these foods if they are actually hungry. Avoid very sweet or salty

foods that are tempting to eat regardless of hunger. Granola bars, protein bars, cheddar crackers, pretzels, popcorn, potato or vegetable chips or "straws," flavored yogurt and "puffs" are some of the worst offenders. The occasional serving of fresh or frozen fruit is fine, but it is best served with something less sweet like peanut butter or plain yogurt.

2. The snack should be eaten seated at a table, not in a car seat or stroller, while watching TV or any other inappropriate location. It is a formal event with a start and a finish. Grazing all morning or afternoon is never appropriate. For sample schedules at all ages, refer to the Quick Guide at the beginning of this book.

EATING TOGETHER

As I mentioned in the last chapter, it is incredibly important that children eat with other people. Many daycares now feed toddlers at communal tables, which is excellent. Yet at home it seems that children often eat alone while mom and dad run around tidying, cooking or otherwise preparing for the day. If at all possible, try to arrange your schedule to allow for at least one or two meals a day at the table with your child. Do not get them seated until all of the food is ready. Serve the same meal to everyone. Talk, laugh, smile and compliment your own cooking. This does not have to be a long, drawn out ordeal – in fact, I doubt your toddler would tolerate that! But try to sit for at least 10–15 minutes and truly eat together. Be sure to turn off all screens, including TVs and smartphones. Consider playing your child's favorite music in the background to create a fun, relaxing atmosphere.

The more you stick with a mealtime routine, the less trouble your child will give you. That being said, kids will be kids. If they are refusing their food or causing a ruckus, push them away from the table to avoid spills and general destruction, but insist that they remain seated until everyone else is finished. I strongly recommend keeping toddlers in a booster seat with a waist strap until they are three or four years old to avoid them getting up and down all throughout the meal. Never offer alternative foods or a backup meal after everyone else is done. You will probably suffer through a few meals to the soundtrack of toddler wails, but in the long run, this strategy produces kids who understand how meals work.

Remember, there is always another meal just a few hours away, and you will all survive until then.

BALANCED MEALS

The government has tried (and failed) for years to educate the public on what a "balanced diet" should look like. Sadly, the Dietary Guidelines for Americans, as they are currently called, are driven more by politics than science.[26] Take the old Food Guide Pyramid, for example.[27] Introduced in 1992, it prominently featured what appears to be a giant loaf of white bread, a big bowl of noodles and some saltine crackers as the *foundation* for healthy eating! It went on to put fruits and vegetables on an equal playing field, despite fruit providing substantially more sugar for the same amount of vitamins and minerals. Animal foods are all lumped together, with no distinction in how they were raised or prepared, and all forms of fat are completely demonized despite naturally occurring fatty acids being absolutely critical for good health. The pyramid has since been abandoned for newer, but equally unsubstantiated, versions.[28] My advice is to ignore them all and think about balancing your family's meals in a different way altogether.

First and foremost, you should be serving three meals per day. If there is a large gap between two of the meals, you might offer one snack, but it should be treated much like a mini-meal. All meals and snacks should have a beginning and an end and be eaten at a table or some other formal setting (family picnics are adorable; eating on the couch or in a stroller is not). Each meal or snack should contain the following elements: a protein source, a fat source and a fiber source.

Protein Sources	Fat Sources	Fiber Sources
Best • Meat of any kind – beef, chicken, pork, turkey, etc. • Fish or shellfish of any kind – salmon, tuna, cod, trout, shrimp, crab, etc. • Eggs Good • Yogurt, cottage cheese, cream cheese or cheese • Nuts or nut butter OK • Beans, including tofu and hummus	Best • Olive oil, butter, coconut oil or avocado oil that you used to cook the food, or as a spread or dressing on top of the food • Fatty cuts of meat such as 80/20 ground beef, chicken or turkey thighs and legs with skin, New York strip, ribeye, pork ribs, pork chops, etc. • Fatty fish such as salmon, fresh tuna, anchovies, sardines, etc. • Eggs with the yolk included • Whole milk (3–5% fat) yogurt and cottage cheese, and regular (not low fat) cream cheese and cheese • Fatty fruit: avocado, coconut, olives Good • Nuts or nut butter	Best • Non-starchy vegetables: asparagus, broccoli, brussels sprouts, carrots, cauliflower, celery, green beans, mushrooms, peppers, salad greens and cooking greens, tomatoes, winter squash, zucchini, etc. • Fatty fruit: avocado, coconut, olives Good • Sweet fruit • Starchy vegetables: potatoes and sweet potatoes • Nuts • Beans OK • Brown rice • Corn • Oats • 100% whole wheat breads, pastas, crackers, buns, etc.

At every meal or snack, you should be able to say you provided something from each column above. And of course you can provide more than one thing from each column as well. Doing this will ensure that meals are satisfying and balanced, in and of themselves. It is altogether possible that your toddler will ignore one part or another, or perhaps the whole meal, and that is fine. Just keep providing items from each category and trust your child to eat what he/she needs at that time.

Of course, it is also good to look beyond each individual meal at the overall diet. The key here is *variety*. It would be very easy to get into a rut serving the same handful of technically balanced meals over and over again, especially if they are things you know your toddler is likely to eat. But this not only leads to a diet lower in certain vitamins and minerals, it limits your child's palate to a select few foods. For starters, try to lean more heavily on the items listed under "Best" in the table above, particularly with regard to the fiber category. It is amazing how easy it is for whole grains to be the fiber source at all three meals – oatmeal for breakfast, a sandwich for lunch and brown rice at dinner, for example. At the very least, offer a non-starchy vegetable at two or three meals in addition to the grain food. Even better, try leaving grains out altogether for one or two meals a day. Similarly, try not to offer sweet fruit more than once or twice a day, as it can quickly become the only item your child wants to eat.

FOOD QUALITY

Food quality is perhaps the most complicated topic in this entire book. The modern food supply is a complex hybrid of time-honored farming tradition and newfangled science. Everything from soil quality and fertilization practices to food storage and processing has changed in the past century. As a dietitian, this is not my area of expertise, but it is certainly an area of interest. In my practice, I try to combine what I have learned from the literature with what I know about my patients and their unique circumstances. While my heart (and much of the literature) says that everyone should eat local meat and produce, all grown using traditional farming methods on well-cared-for soil, I know that this is not always practical. So I tend to break down food quality into layers, helping my patients make the best decisions for them in that moment.

Meat

Best	Grass-fed (cows) or pasture-raised (chickens, pigs, turkeys), ideally in organic pastures with organic supplemental feed if needed.
Good	Organic animals raised in confinement or non-organic animals that were grass-fed/pasture raised.
OK	Non-organic animals raised in confinement.
Avoid	Any processed meat product with added fillers, chemicals, breading, etc. Always buy pure, plain meat or meat with a very basic list of seasonings that you could easily replicate at home, if desired.

Eggs

Best	Fresh eggs from chickens living on pasture. They will be freshest if you have the chance to buy locally, but many grocery stores also carry pasture-raised eggs from areas of the country with a temperate climate year-round.
Good	Organic eggs are a good choice at the grocery store. Opt for the cheapest organic eggs you can find. All organic eggs are held to the same standards with regard to non-GMO feed, animal welfare standards and antibiotic use. Terms like "free-range" and "cage-free" are not as regulated, and the benefits they do confer are so minimal that it is unlikely they lead to a more nutritious egg. Similarly, brown eggs are simply produced by certain breeds of chicken – they are in no way inherently healthier.
OK	Any grocery store egg.
Avoid	Cartons of egg whites or other liquid egg blends. Always buy whole eggs (and eat the yolks)!

FISH

Best	Wild-caught fish and shellfish.
Good	Farm-raised fish that is responsibly and sustainably farmed. Unfortunately, there is not currently a verification system that helps consumers quickly determine which farms are meeting higher standards. One thing you can do is research the farm online, or speak directly with your fishmonger.
OK	Farm-raised fish from farms with poor aquaponics practices, such as antibiotic or fungicide use.
Avoid	Any processed fish product with added fillers, chemicals, breading, etc. Always buy pure, plain fish or fish with a very basic list of seasonings that you could easily replicate at home, if desired.

MILK, CHEESE & YOGURT

Best	Much like beef, milk is most nutritious if it comes from grass-fed cows raised on pasture. If you have the ability to buy milk and milk products from a local farmer, that is fantastic. If not, many grass-fed dairy products are popping up on grocery store shelves. Always choose whole milk products for the whole family. Whole milk is approximately 3.5% fat, which is the natural fat content of cow's milk. This fat will help kids and adults alike to absorb the nutrition in the milk, yogurt or cheese.
Good	Organic dairy products are also a good option, as this ensures that the animal was fed organic, non-GMO feed and was not given hormones or antibiotics.
OK	Non-organic dairy products.
Avoid	Skim milk, fat-free yogurt, flavored milks and yogurts, American cheese.

GRAINS

As I have mentioned already, grains and grain products are not very nutritious and should not make up the bulk of your child's diet. However, when you do choose to serve them, it is important to serve high-quality, unprocessed whole grains.

Good	Sprouted grains. Sprouted grains are whole grains that have been allowed to germinate. This process makes the nutrients in grains much more available for digestion and use. You can find sprouted brown rice and sprouted rolled oats online and at select health food stores. You can also find breads, crackers, pastas and more that are made with 100% sprouted wheat, corn, rice and oats.
OK	Whole grains. Whole grains contain three key parts: bran (mostly fiber), germ (mostly vitamins and minerals) and endosperm (mostly carbohydrate). By choosing whole grains, you will get a more complete nutritional package. Brown rice, oats and corn are all good whole grain choices. Wheat products such as breads, crackers, pastas and buns can be acceptable if made with 100% whole wheat flour.
Avoid	Refined grains. Avoid foods made with refined grains, namely refined wheat. Refined wheat is used to make all-purpose flour, often called enriched wheat flour or white flour on ingredient labels. Manufacturers use refined wheat flour to make the vast majority of commercially available breads, crackers, pastas, buns and baked goods. Also avoid cereal, which despite being made with some whole grains, is highly processed and almost always sweetened with sugar.

Fruits & Vegetables

Once upon a time, *all* fruits and vegetables were organic.[29] It is somewhat amazing that "organic" produce is now thought of as special, considering it is essentially just the original way of growing things. Imagine a store where all the organic produce was unmarked, but any produce grown with pesticides, fertilizers or bioengineering was marked as such. It might change the way people think about things! Unfortunately, what it likely would *not* change is the price differential. Organic farming, especially on a large scale, is simply more laborious and expensive than modern methods. For that reason, I often refer patients to the Environmental Working Group's (EWG) "Dirty Dozen" and "Clean Fifteen" lists in order to help them decide where to shell out extra money and where to pinch their pennies.[30]

EWG Dirty Dozen	These fruits and vegetables, when conventionally grown, have the highest load of pesticide residues. If possible, buy organic.	Strawberries, spinach, kale, nectarines, apples, grapes, peaches, cherries, pears, tomatoes, celery, potatoes.
EWG Clean Fifteen	These fruits and vegetables are least likely to contain pesticide residues even if they were grown using conventional practices.	Avocados, sweet corn, pineapples, frozen sweet peas, onions, papayas, eggplants, asparagus, kiwis, cabbages, cauliflower, cantaloupes, broccoli, mushrooms, honeydew melon.

Special Treats

One of the greatest joys of parenting is watching your child's eyes light up when they taste something truly delicious. Special, sweet treats are deeply woven into our culture and I am not here to rip that away from you. As a parent, you have the unique and powerful opportunity to teach your child the definition of "special." What classifies as special is intensely personal, but the challenge is the same for all of us – drawing the line. I can say with authority that the line is stricter than daily treats. Despite the modern-day insistence that every lunch deserves a cookie and every dinner is followed by dessert, that simply is not appropriate. Your job is to help your child differentiate between a special day and a regular day. Help them understand the beauty of homespun treats made from time-honored family recipes versus store-bought, dime-a-dozen desserts and candy. And perhaps most importantly, do not constantly reference health and nutrition as the reason we typically avoid sweet and decadent foods. Instead, shift the focus to how special these foods are, and how much fun it is to make them together and eat them on extraordinary days.

AFTERWORD

If you are reading this book, you are most likely a parent, or about to be one, and you are probably starting to realize that you have a monumental task on your hands. Parenting in the 21st century is unlike anything that humans have experienced before. Human scientific knowledge is skyrocketing and readily accessible to the masses, yet our food supply continues to deteriorate as we try to make everything simultaneously cheap, convenient, accessible and profitable. And amongst all this confusion and complexity, you are just one parent, sitting in your house, gazing into the eyes of a tiny human who is relying on you for absolutely everything. Take a deep breath and know that you *can* eke some control out of the whirlwind that is modern-day parenting. Perhaps you can breastfeed for a little longer. Or maybe you can make a delicious liver pâté for your six-month-old. You might be able to rearrange your schedule a bit to establish family mealtimes. These small, manageable steps are all part of a bigger success story. Start now, and before you know it, you will be sitting at the table, gazing into those same eyes attached to a much older, wiser and robustly healthy man or woman and know that you did it: your healthy little foodie is all grown up.

REFERENCES

1. Centers for Disease Control and Prevention. (2017, July 18). New CDC report: More than 100 million Americans have diabetes or prediabetes. Retrieved from https://www.cdc.gov/media/releases/2017/p0718-diabetes-report.html

2. Centers for Disease Control and Prevention. (2019, April 29). Childhood obesity facts. Retrieved from https://www.cdc.gov/healthyschools/obesity/facts.htm

3. Moss, M. (2013, February 20). The extraordinary science of addictive junk food. The New York Times Magazine. Retrieved from https://www.nytimes.com/2013/02/24/magazine/the-extraordinary-science-of-junk-food.html

4. Hoecker, J.L. (2019, April 20). When's the right time to start feeding a baby solid foods? Retrieved from https://www.mayoclinic.org/healthy-lifestyle/infant-and-toddler-health/expert-answers/starting-solids/faq-20057889

5. Heaney, R. P. (2005). The vitamin D requirement in health and disease. Journal of Steroid Biochemistry and Molecular Biology, 97(1–2), 13–9. doi: 10.1016/j.jsbmb.2005.06.020

6. World Health Organization. (2001). Complementary feeding: Report of the global consultation, and summary of guiding principles for complementary feeding of the breastfed child. Retrieved from https://apps.who.int/iris/handle/10665/42739

7. Gartner, L. M., Morton, J., Lawrence, R.A., Naylor, A. J., O'Hare, D., Schanler, R. J., Eidelman, A. I. (2005). Breastfeeding and the use of human milk.

Journal of Pediatrics, 115(2), 496–506. doi: 10.1542/peds.2004-2491

8. Centers for Disease Control and Prevention. (2016). Breastfeeding report card. Retrieved from https://www.cdc.gov/breastfeeding/pdf/2016breastfeedingreportcard.pdf

9. Perrine, C. G., Sharma, A. J., Jefferds, M. E. D., Serdula, M. K., Scanlon, K. S. (2010). Adherence to Vitamin D recommendations among US infants. Journal of Pediatrics, 125(4), 627. doi: 10.1542/peds.2009-2571

10. Holick, M. F. (2004). Sunlight and vitamin D for bone health and prevention of autoimmune diseases, cancers, and cardiovascular disease. American Journal of Clinical Nutrition, 80(6), 1678S–1688S. doi: 10.1093/ajcn/80.6.1678S

11. Lupo, K. D., Schmitt, D. N. (1997). Experiments in bone boiling: Nutritional returns and archaeological reflections. Anthropozoologica, N(25–26), 137–144. Retrieved from http://sciencepress.mnhn.fr/sites/default/files/articles/pdf/az1998n25-26a15.pdf

12. Daniel, K. (2003, June 18). Why broth is beautiful: Essential roles for proline, glycine and gelatin. Retrieved from https://www.westonaprice.org/health-topics/why-broth-is-beautiful-essential-roles-for-proline-glycine-and-gelatin/

13. Daniels, L., Heath, A. M., Williams, S. M., Cameron, S. L., Fleming, E. A., Taylor, B. J., Wheeler, B. J., Gibson, R. S., Taylor, R. W. (2015). Baby-Led Introduction to SolidS (BLISS) study: A randomised controlled trial of a baby-led approach to

complementary feeding. BMC Pediatrics, 15, 179. doi: 10.1186/s12887-015-0491-8

14. National Institute of Allergy and Infectious Disease. (2017). Addendum guidelines for the prevention of peanut allergy in the United States. Retrieved from https://www.niaid.nih.gov/sites/default/files/peanut-allergy-prevention-guidelines-parent-summary.pdf

15. Dewey, K. G. (2013). The challenge of meeting nutrient needs of infants and young children during the period of complementary feeding: An evolutionary perspective. Journal of Nutrition, 143(12), 2050–2054. doi: 10.3945/jn.113.182527

16. Björn-Rasmussen, E., Hallberg, L., Isaksson, B., Arvidsson, B. (1974). Food iron absorption in man: Applications of the two-pool extrinsic tag method to measure heme and nonheme iron absorption from the whole diet. Journal of Clinical Investigation, 53, 247–255. doi: 10.1172/JCI107545

17. Simopoulos, A. P. (2006). Evolutionary aspects of diet, the omega-6/omega-3 ratio and genetic variation: Nutritional implications for chronic diseases. Journal of Biomedicine and Pharmacotherapy, 60(9), 502–507. doi: 10.1016/j.biopha.2006.07.080

18. Lemmens, L., Van Buggenhout, S., Oey, I., Van Loey, A., Hendrickx, M. (2009). Towards a better understanding of the relationship between the β-carotene in vitro bio-accessibility and pectin structural changes: A case study on carrots. Food Research International, 42(9), 1323–1330. doi: 10.1016/j.foodres.2009.04.006

19. Rabbani, G. H., Teka, T., Saha, S. K., Zaman, B., Majid, N., Khatun, M., Wahed, M. A., Fuchs, G. J. (2004). Green banana and pectin improve small

intestinal permeability and reduce fluid loss in Bangladeshi children with persistent diarrhea. Journal of Digestive Diseases and Sciences, 49(3), 475–484. doi: 10.1023/B:DDAS.0000020507.25910.cf

20. Lever, E., Cole, J., Scott, S. M., Emery, P. W., Whelan, K. (2014). Systematic review: The effect of prunes on gastrointestinal function. Journal of Alimentary Pharmacology and Therapeutics, 40(7), 750–758. doi: 10.1111/apt.12913

21. Awika, J. M. (2011). Advances in cereal science: Implications to food processing and health promotion (pp. 1–13). Washington, DC: American Chemical Society.

22. Oliveira, A. C., Pordeus, I. A., Torres, C. S., Martins, M. T., Paiva, S. M. (2010). Feeding and nonnutritive sucking habits and prevalence of open bite and crossbite in children/adolescents with Down syndrome. Angle Orthodontist, 80(4), 748–753. doi: 10.2319/072709-421.1

23. Hoppe, C., Mølgaard, C., Vaag, A., Barkholt, V., Michaelsen, K. F. (2005). High intakes of milk, but not meat, increase s-insulin and insulin resistance in 8-year-old boys. European Journal of Clinical Nutrition, 59, 393–398. doi: 10.1038/sj.ejcn.1602086

24. Ludwig, D. D., Willett, W. C. (2013). Three daily servings of reduced-fat milk: An evidence-based recommendation? JAMA Pediatrics, 167(9), 788–789. doi: 10.1001/jamapediatrics.2013.2408

25. Iacono, G., Cavataio, F., Montalto, G., Florena, A. (1998). Intolerance of cow's milk and chronic constipation in children. New England Journal of Medicine, 339, 1100–1104. doi: 10.1056/NEJM199810153391602

26. Nestle, M. (2007). Food politics: How the food industry influences nutrition and health (revised and expanded ed.). Berkeley and Los Angeles, CA: University of California Press.

27. Office of Disease Prevention and Health Promotion. (n.d.). Retrieved from https://health.gov/dietaryguidelines/dga2000/document/build.htm

28. Office of Disease Prevention and Health Promotion. (n.d.). Retrieved from https://health.gov/dietaryguidelines/

29. Kerr Center for Sustainable Agriculture. (2010). A brief overview of the history and philosophy of organic agriculture. Retrieved from http://kerrcenter.com/wp-content/uploads/2014/08/organic-philosophy-report.pdf

30. Environmental Working Group. (2019). EWG's 2019 shopper's guide to pesticides in produce. Retrieved from https://www.ewg.org/foodnews/summary.php